OVER 150 JOKES
FROM
CAMP FUNNY-HA-HA

BY
TERI JAMES-BRUMLEY

Pictures by Jerry Zimmerman

Published by The Trumpet Club
666 Fifth Avenue, New York, New York 10103

Copyright © 1990 by Dell Publishing, a division of
Bantam Doubleday Dell Publishing Group, Inc.

ISBN: 0-440-84270-0

Printed in the United States of America
September 1990

10 9 8 7 6 5 4 3
OPM

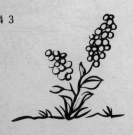

For the kids of Winsor Place:
Millicent, Will, Brittany, Schuyler,
Manu, Rebecca, and Jack

DAILY DELIRIUM

WELCOME, CAMPERS

At Camp Funny-Ha-Ha our motto is Wampum Stompum Sillium (Indian for "Rolling Bears Are Silly"). To participate in any of our delirious daily activities, you must first pass the laughter test. If you can read the following book without one snicker, you will most assuredly not make it through the front gate!

REVEILLE!
MEET YOUR BUNKMATES

BERTHA CRUMP
Girls' Head Counselor

INDIAN NICKNAME: Big Foot (She wears a size 11!)

FAVORITE ACTIVITY: Waterskiing, because she doesn't have to use skis

PET PEEVE: Campers using her sneakers as canoes

BIFF ARMSTRONG III
Boys' Head Counselor

INDIAN NICKNAME: Big Bucks

FAVORITE ACTIVITY: Counting his father's money

PET PEEVE: Mud splatters on his tennis shorts

ELEANOR ILL
Camper

INDIAN NICKNAME: Running Nose

FAVORITE ACTIVITY: Asking the nurse to take her temperature

PET PEEVE: Cold stethoscopes

LEON R. COWARD
Camper

INDIAN NICKNAME:	Running Scared
FAVORITE ACTIVITY:	Hiding under the covers
PET PEEVE:	Ghost stories, spiders, and public speaking (which includes singing around the campfire)

DENNIS DO-LITTLE
Camper

INDIAN NICKNAME: Sleeping Bear

FAVORITE ACTIVITY: Rest hour

PET PEEVE: Reveille – and being asked to do anything

GABBY GILDENSTERN
Camper

INDIAN NICKNAME:	Rolling Tongue
FAVORITE ACTIVITY:	Gossiping
PET PEEVE:	No telephones at camp so she has to use her portable fax machine to talk to her friends back home

DARLENE DITZ
Camper

INDIAN NICKNAME: Feather Head

FAVORITE ACTIVITY: Basket weaving

PET PEEVE: Toasting marshmallows with a toothpick (and she wonders why she's always setting her hand on fire)

I. M. BEST
Camper

INDIAN NICKNAME:	Hooting Owl
FAVORITE ACTIVITY:	Being right all the time
PET PEEVE:	Being wrong ever

LAKESIDE LAUGHTER

GABBY: Where do cantaloupes go in the summer?

DENNIS: John Cougar Melon-camp.

GABBY: Why is the forest always so noisy?

DENNIS: Every tree has its own bark.

GABBY: What has twelve feet, green hair, and purple teeth?

DENNIS: I don't know.

GABBY: I don't know either, but there's one crawling up your neck.

GABBY: What's the driest day of the week?
DENNIS: Thirst-day.

GABBY: What's the hottest day of the week?
DENNIS: Fry-day.

GABBY: What's the best day to have dessert?
DENNIS: Sun-dae.

GABBY: Knock, knock.
DENNIS: Who's there?
GABBY: The Invisible Man.
DENNIS: Tell him I can't see him right now.

GABBY: Knock, knock.
DENNIS: Who's there?
GABBY: Celeste.
DENNIS: Celeste who?
GABBY: Celeste.
DENNIS: Celeste who!
GABBY: Celeste time I'll knock on your tent.

GABBY: Did you hear that the camp canoe ran into a sharkway?
DENNIS: No. What's a sharkway?
GABBY: About 90 pounds!

GABBY: What time is it when an elephant sits on your tent?

DENNIS: Time to get a new tent.

GABBY: Why should you avoid the woods from two to four?

DENNIS: Because that's when the elephants practice jumping out of the trees.

GABBY: What happened to your mouth?

DENNIS: I just ate a toasted marshmallow.

GABBY: Huh?

DENNIS: It was still on fire!

GABBY: Do you know the difference between a raisin and a tarantula?

DENNIS: No.

GABBY: Remind me never to send you to the camp store.

GABBY: Why did the chicken cross the lake?

DENNIS: I don't know.

GABBY: To get the *Hiawatha Times*.

DENNIS: Huh?

GABBY: Don't you get it?

DENNIS: No.

GABBY: Neither do I. I get the *New York Post*.

GABBY: What's a ringleader?
DENNIS: The first one in the bathtub.

GABBY: Why did the doctor send Eleanor home from camp?
DENNIS: Because he thought she was two tents (tense).

GABBY: Which planet reminds you of a circus?
DENNIS: Saturn. It has three rings.

GABBY: What planet can you see without a telescope?
DENNIS: The planet Earth.

GABBY: You can have the top bunk.
DENNIS: No thanks, I don't like to oversleep.

GABBY: Will you remember me a year from now?
DENNIS: Of course.
GABBY: Will you remember me a month from now?
DENNIS: Sure.
GABBY: Will you remember me a week from now?
DENNIS: Absolutely.
GABBY: Knock, knock.
DENNIS: Who's there?
GABBY: I thought you said you'd remember me.

BUGGY BELLY LAUGHS

What's a mosquito's favorite sport?
Skin diving.

What goes snap, crackle, pop?
A firefly with a short circuit.

What are the most famous insects?
The Beatles.

What does a bee like to chew?
Bumble gum.

What do you call a baby insect?
An inf-ant.

What do you get when you cross a builder
with a bug?
A carpenter ant.

What are the biggest insects?
Gi-ants.

What are the smartest insects?
Fireflies – because they're so bright.

What insect melts on hot summer days?
A butter-fly.

Can insects cry?
**Sure, haven't you seen a moth bawl
(mothball)?**

What insect is the most musical?
A hum-bug.

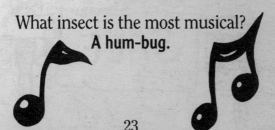

What did the moth say when it got too close to the lantern?
That really burns me up.

What insect sleeps the most?
A bed-bug.

Where's the best place to buy bugs?
At a flea market.

MESS-HALL MANIA

BERTHA: Hey, there's a fly in my soup!

BIFF: Don't worry, the spider on your bread will take care of it.

BERTHA: The sign over the Mess-Hall door makes me nervous.

BIFF: Why, what does it say?

BERTHA: Eat here and you'll never live to regret it.

BERTHA: Do you know what a pickle is?

BIFF: Yeah, something you eat on a hamburger.

BERTHA: No, it's a cucumber in a sour mood.

BERTHA: What's wrinkled, grows on vines, and is very dangerous?

BIFF: A raisin with a machine gun.

BERTHA: What food sounds cool but can really burn you up?

BIFF: Chili.

BERTHA: What did one hot dog say to the other hot dog?

BIFF: Hi, Frank.

BERTHA: What's gray and lumpy and comes in a can?

BIFF: Cream of elephant soup.

BERTHA: What are an elephant's favorite foods?

BIFF: Peanut butter and squash.

BERTHA: What did the mayonnaise say to the refrigerator?

BIFF: Close the door, I'm dressing.

BERTHA: What do sheep like to eat?

BIFF: Baa-nanas.

BERTHA: What did one potato chip say to the other at the party?

BIFF: Want to go for a dip?

BERTHA: Why did the baker stop making doughnuts for breakfast?

BIFF: He was tired of the hole business.

BERTHA: Why are potatoes such good detectives?

BIFF: Because they keep their eyes peeled.

BERTHA: What did the raisin say to the cinnamon bagel?

BIFF: I'm rolling in dough.

BERTHA: What is rhubarb?

BIFF: Celery with high blood pressure.

BERTHA: What do coffee and dirt have in common?

BIFF: They're both ground.

BERTHA: What did the fork say to the spoon?

BIFF: Who's that sharp guy next to you?

BERTHA: What's a lazy camper's favorite food?

BIFF: Turkey loaf.

BERTHA: Why are grapes never lonely?

BIFF: Because they hang around in bunches.

BERTHA: What did the strawberry say to the peanut?

BIFF: Help me! I'm in a jam.

BERTHA: Why did the ice cream dive into the lake?

BIFF: It wanted to take a dip.

INFIRMARY INSANITY

ELEANOR: What do you call for help when you
hurt your toe?

LEON: A toe truck.

ELEANOR: What is the difference between a
doctor and a duck?

LEON: The doctor has a larger bill.

ELEANOR: What do you get when you cross a
comedian with a germ?

LEON: Sick jokes.

ELEANOR: What happens if you fall on a record player?
LEON: You wind up with a slipped disc.

ELEANOR: Why did the house call for a doctor?
LEON: Because it had window pains (panes).

ELEANOR: What disease is a horse most likely to get?
LEON: Hay fever.

ELEANOR: Knock, knock.
LEON: Who's there?
ELEANOR: Amnesia.
LEON: Amnesia who?
ELEANOR: Oh, I see you have it too.

ELEANOR: What bug is good for your health?
LEON: Vitamin Bee.

ELEANOR: What do most books and all babies have in common?
LEON: Each one comes with an appendix.

ELEANOR: Doctor, doctor.
DOCTOR: What?
ELEANOR: Every time I take a sip of my chocolate milk, I get a sharp pain in my eye.
DOCTOR: Next time take the straw out before you drink it.

ELEANOR: Doctor, doctor.
DOCTOR: Yes?
ELEANOR: After the operation will I be able to ride a horse?
DOCTOR: Of course.
ELEANOR: That's funny, I never could before.

ELEANOR: Doctor, doctor.
DOCTOR: Yes?
ELEANOR: I think my ankle is broke.
DOCTOR: How do you know – did you check its wallet?

ELEANOR: What state is always sick?
LEON: Ill.

ELEANOR: What state could make Ill. better?
LEON: Md.

ELEANOR: Doctor, doctor.
DOCTOR: Yes?
ELEANOR: I lost my appetite.
DOCTOR: We better send out a search party.

ELEANOR: Doctor, doctor.
DOCTOR: What?
ELEANOR: My bunkmate thinks she's a chicken.
DOCTOR: That's terrible. Why didn't you come see me sooner?
ELEANOR: I would have but we needed the eggs for breakfast.

PATHETIC ATHLETICS

Why is it helpful to have a baseball player
along when you go camping?
In case you need someone to pitch the tent.

What one vegetable would you rather not
have in your canoe?
A leek.

What has eighteen legs, red spots, and
catches flies?
A baseball team with the measles.

What traffic violation is allowed in baseball?
Hit and run.

What is the best place for a track star to
wash his shoes?
In running water.

Why did the bowling pins lie down?
They were on strike.

What bird is useful to have around during a
boxing match?
A duck.

Why are fish such poor tennis players?
They don't like to get too close to the net.

What is a frog's favorite game?
Hopscotch.

What game do baby chickens play?
Peck-a-boo.

Why did the doctor take bandages to the
card game?
In case someone cut the deck.

What game do ghouls play?
Corpse and robbers.

Why did the camper take his winter coat to
the baseball game?
**He heard there were going to be a thousand
fans there.**

When is football like a refund?
When you get a quarterback.

What did the worm say to the camper when
he went fishing?
I'm hooked on you.

NUTTY NATURE

Why does Mrs. Owl worry about her son?
Because he doesn't give a hoot.

Why do bears sleep for six months?
Who would dare wake a bear!

How can you tell if an elephant is sleeping
in your tent?
His breath smells like peanut butter.

What does a skunk do when he gets mad?
He raises a stink.

How do rabbits travel?
By hare-plane.

How do you know that carrots are good for
your eyes?
Have you ever seen a rabbit wearing glasses?

Where do frogs hang up their coats?
In the croak room.

Is the camp's pony very sick?
No, he's just a little hoarse.

What is wind?
Air in a hurry.

What do you get when you cross a cat with
a tree?
A cat-a-log.

How do you tell a fish you like him?
Drop him a line.

What did the puddle say to the rain?
Drop in sometime.

What has four legs and goes oom oom?
A cow walking backwards.

What has six eyes and still cannot see?
Three blind mice.

How do you get down off a horse?
You don't, you get down off a goose.

What's the best way to keep a skunk from smelling?
Hold its nose.

What's the best way to catch a squirrel?
Hide in a tree and act like a nut.

How do you stop a herd of rhinos from charging?
Take away their credit cards.

What kind of bird is the most frightening?
A scare-crow.

How do you make an elephant laugh?
Tell him a rhinoceros joke.

SING-ALONG SILLINESS

STRAIGHT UP
(Are We Gonna Be on This Hike Forever?)

to the tune of "Straight Up"
music by Elliot Wolff
originally performed by Paula Abdul

Lost in the woods,
I don't know just why we're here.
The signs don't look too good,
That we'll never return is my fear.

Chorus:
We've walked by here before,
I feel like throwin' myself down on the forest
floor.
Could we just take a break now – PLEASE!
Straight up, now tell me,
Are we gonna be on this hike forever?
Oh, oh, oh.
When are we gonna get back?
Straight up, now tell me,
Since we're all on this hike together,
Oh, oh, oh,
Please carry my backpack!

I'm standin' still.
No more steps will I take.
I've had my fill.
I think that it's time for a break.

Chorus:
We've walked by here before,
I feel like throwin' myself down on the forest
 floor.
Could we just take a break now – PLEASE!
Straight up, now tell me,
Are we gonna be on this hike forever?
Oh, oh, oh.
When are we gonna get back?
Straight up, now tell me,
Since we're all on this hike together,
Oh, oh, oh.
Please carry my backpack!

These bugs are eatin' me,
They fly right up to me,
With their rude intentions.
My feet are killin' me,
I feel that I could –
Die, die, die, die, die, die, die, die, die.

Could we go home now?
Could we go home now?
Could we go home now?

We've walked by here before,
I feel like throwin' myself down on the forest
  floor.
Could you find a chair for me?
Or will my death end up in a mystery book?
I don't mean to make demands,
But a little rest would feel so grand.
How about a little break now – PLEASE!

THEY CALL ME LAZY

to the tune of "She Drives Me Crazy"
music by and originally performed by
Fine Young Cannibals

There is no doubt I like to sleep.
But that don't make me a creep.
They wake us up each morning.
I wish they would give some warning.
6 A.M. is too early.
And it just makes me surly.

Chorus:
They call me lazy, like no one else.
They call me lazy, and I can't help myself.

This all makes me distressed.
If I don't sleep I get depressed.
Don't know what I'm gonna do.
It makes me want to boo hoo hoo.
I wish they would let me slumber.
This early hour is not my number.

Chorus:
They call me lazy, like no one else.
They call me lazy, and I can't help myself.

NOT TOO ROUGH

to the tune of "Hangin' Tough"
music by Maurice Starr
performed by New Kids on the Block

Oh, oh, oh, oh, oh.
Oh, oh, oh, oh, oh.
Oh, oh, oh, oh, oh.
Oh, oh, oh, oh, oh.

Listen up, everybody, it's time to do aerobics!
You'd think that we were all exercise-a-phobics!
Don't worry 'bout nothin', it'll be such fun.
'Cuz you're gonna feel a lot better when we're
    all done!

'Cuz it's really,
Not too rough!
Not too rough!
Not too rough!
Are you tough enough?
Not too rough!
Not too rough!
Not too rough!
We're tough!

Everybody's always talking 'bout who's too fat!
Just get off your butt and do somethin' 'bout that!
We ain't gonna cut anybody any slack!
Just get up and move and get on the right track!

Oh, oh, oh, oh, oh.
Oh, oh, oh, oh, oh.
Oh, oh, oh, oh, oh.
Oh, oh, oh, oh, oh.

Get juiced everybody 'cuz we're gonna exercise!
'Cuz we gotta getcha movin' to bring down
    your size!

'Cuz it's really,
Not too rough!
Not too rough!
Not too rough!
Are you tough enough?
Not too rough!
Not too rough!
Not too rough!
We're tough!

COLD-HEARTED (LAKE)

to the tune of "Cold-Hearted"
music by Elliot Wolff
originally performed by Paula Abdul

Chorus:
It's a cold-hearted lake,
Hope we don't capsize.
Oh, oh.
Please don't be so wise.
This is not the place to play,
This ain't no heated pool.
Oh, oh.
Please don't play the fool – no.

You're the one dishin' out the splashes,
With your paddle flashin'.
Here I am in back, it seems, the only drip in
   this canoe.
You're the one not pad-dl-ing,
You are such a slacker.
You just leave me all the work, this is plainly true.

Chorus:
It's a cold-hearted lake,
Hope we don't capsize.
Oh, oh.
Please don't be so wise.
This is not the place to play,
This ain't no heated pool.
Oh, oh.
Please don't play the fool – no.

In the middle of the lake,
You have got me freakin'.
I have only just one wish, that you would please
    just settle down.
Through the whole canoe trip,
You've been up there geekin'.
When it comes to real dweebs, with you there is
    no match.

I should make you swim all the way back.
You can really make me mad,
And I will if you make one more crack.
This lake's as cold as ice....
C-c-c-cold-hearted lake,
C-c-c-cold-hearted lake....

Repeat Chorus.

A WHITE DUFF*

to the tune of "You Got It (The Right Stuff)"
music by Maurice Starr
originally performed by New Kids on the Block

A white duff.
A white duff.

It was well after nightfall,
Right down by the lake shore,
I caught a glimpse of somethin' I'd never seen
    before.

Chorus:
I could see it in the lake,
It made me quake.
I could see it shinin' bright like the moon,
In the month of June.
I saw a white duff, baby,
Bobbin' in the lake last night.
I saw a white duff, baby,
Floatin' in the pale moonlight.

*Duff is a Midwestern term for a person's backside. Of course, if you are
  from the Midwest, you already knew that.

48

Could not see just who it was,
The light was not right.
But I was delighted because
    I'd tell all (back at the camp).

Oh, oh, oh, oh, oh. Oh, oh, oh, oh.
Oh, oh, oh, oh, oh. A white duff.
Oh, oh, oh, oh, oh. Oh, oh, oh, oh.
Oh, oh, oh, oh, oh. A white duff.

I ran back to the campsite,
To tell the cause of my delight.
Come see some skinny-dippers in the pale
    moonlight.

Repeat Chorus.

LIGHTS OUT: GHOULISH FOOLISHNESS

What is a ghost's favorite carnival ride?
A roller ghoster.

What do monsters eat for breakfast?
Dreaded Wheat.

If Dracula, Werewolf, Jason, and Freddy all
showed up in your tent on the same day,
what would you do?
Hope it was Halloween!

What did one ghost say to the other ghost?
Do you believe in people?

Where do spooks buy stamps?
At the ghost office.

Why did the vampire avoid sleeping campers?
Because he didn't like tired blood.

How does a witch tell time?
With her witch watch.

Why do ghosts hang out in bars?
Because they're one of the few places that serve spirits.

What town is considered the ghost capital of the world?
Casper, Wyoming.

What do you call the area where ghosts and goblins live?
A terror-tory.

How does a modern witch travel?
By vacuum cleaner.

What kind of spook can be found both in the desert and by the sea?
A sand-witch.

How does a monster predict his future?
With his horror-scope.

What's the best way to get rid of a spook?
Exorcise a lot.

What do ghosts wear to protect themselves while driving?
Sheet belts.

What kind of pasta do ghosts like best?
Spooketti.

What room is a vampire's favorite?
The bat-room.

What do vampires drive to work?
Bloodmobiles.

What did the camper say to the vampire?
You're a pain in the neck.

What is a witch's favorite dessert?
Ice scream.

What do ghosts eat for breakfast?
Ghost Toasties.

What do monster babies and bugs have in common?
They're both creepy crawlers.

What is a zombie's least favorite room?
The living room.

What kind of horses do you find only in your dreams?
Night-mares.

What do spooks need before they can occupy a house?
A haunting license.

What do vampires take when they have a cold?
Coffin drops.

How do ghosts like their eggs?
Terror-fried.

CAMP FUNNY-HA-HA'S

**The first week at camp,
the following records were set:**

Bertha ate 2,316 toasted marshmallows during
a sing-along.

Dennis identified more than 88 types of mold in the
bread basket.

Gabby's tent sang 11,422 verses of "Row, Row, Row
Your Boat."

Eleanor counted 973 mosquito bites on her ankles.

Leon discovered 63 different types of creepy things
in the shower.

Biff made it through an entire week without getting
his tennis whites dirty.

Darlene got lost 57 times on her way to the
Mess Hall.

HALL OF SHAME

The second week of camp, the following records were set:

Bertha set the record for the longest stomachache ever—3 days, 21 hours, and 37 minutes.

All 67 campers came down with food poisoning.

Gabby's tent had laryngitis for 5 days.

768 flea bites were counted on one camper's face. Unfortunately no one could identify the camper to send her home.

No one took a shower.

66 stains were counted on Biff's clothes after a food fight.

Darlene went without food for 4 days—until she finally found the Mess Hall.

DEAR MOM: LETTERS HOME

The Fool-Proof Letter
*(Just photocopy and fill in the blanks for Mom.
She'll appreciate it.)*

Dear Mom,

Please send *(check one)*:

_____ more money.

_____ more food.

_____ help.

Camp is:

_____ a blast!

_____ okay.

_____ a major bore.

I:

_____ never want to come home.

_____ would consider coming home if you buy
me a new Nintendo cartridge.

_____ want you to come get me NOW!

Love,

_____ *(your name here)*

Dear Mom,

Thanks for the great cookies. After sharing a few around, I was able to get some kid to trade me his Walkman radio for the rest. Please send another 8 or 10 dozen. By the time camp is over, I should have that washer and dryer you want.

Your son the businessman

Dear Mom,

Camp is great. It's been, like, no problem. The first night here, I ate so many s'mores that I didn't sleep all night. Maybe it was the chocolate.

The next day, I was so tired that I took a nap in the woods. Well, it turns out that those little plants, with the three shiny leaves, that I slept on made me itch all over.

That very same night, I fell out of the top bunk when I tried to scratch my big toe.

The doctor says I can go swimming as soon as the cast is off and my scabs heal.

Love,
Itchy

Dear Mom,

Why did you have to sew my
name on the outside of all my
underwear? All the other kids
have their names on the inside.
Boy there sure are a lot of
kids named Fruit-of-the-
Loom around here!

Love,
Your little Ditz

Dear Mom,

My first day at camp I didn't
make any friends.
My second day at camp I made
three enemies.
My third day at camp I made
three friends.
So things are looking up.

XOXOXO

THE CRAZY CAMPER

Why was Ditzy Darlene glad she wasn't a bird?
Because she couldn't fly.

Why did Ditzy Darlene climb the tree?
Because the sign said "Keep off the grass."

Why did Ditzy Darlene throw out her ant farm?
**Because her counselor said the only way she would
get well is to get rid of her bug.**

Why is Ditzy Darlene eating hay?
Because you always say she eats like a horse.

Why did Ditzy Darlene take her yardstick to bed?
Because she wanted to see how long she would sleep.

Why did Ditzy Darlene put the cow in the icebox?
She wanted ice cream.

Why did Ditzy Darlene throw her shoes away?
Because they kept sticking their tongues out at her.

Why did Ditzy Darlene put her bunk in the campfire?
Because she wanted to sleep like a log.

Why does Ditzy Darlene always tiptoe by the infirmary?
So she doesn't wake the sleeping pills.

Why did Ditzy Darlene throw a piece of candy to the drowning camper?
Because it was a Life Saver.

Why did Ditzy Darlene throw her clock out of the tent?
Because she wanted to see time fly.

Why did Ditzy Darlene try to take her nose apart?
Because she wanted to see what made it run.

Why did Ditzy Darlene take fish and bones out into the middle of the lake?
Because she heard it was raining cats and dogs.

Why did Ditzy Darlene dance with the cow?
Because she wanted a milk shake.

Why is Ditzy Darlene all wet?
Because someone told her to go jump in a lake.

GOOFY GOOD-BYES

The Campers' Last Will and Testament

To Bertha, we leave five cases of athlete's-foot powder and two cases of Ultra Slimfast.

To Biff, we leave a bottle of bleach and 225 worthless shares of stock in Camp Funny-Ha-Ha.

To Eleanor, we leave a Band-Aid and Doogie Howser's phone number.

To Leon, we leave a black widow spider and a book by Stephen King.

To Dennis, we leave the book *How To Imitate a Turtle* and a subscription to *Couch Potato* magazine.

To Gabby, we leave two cases of throat lozenges and a gift certificate for a tonsillectomy.

To Darlene, we leave a route map for the Mess Hall and a two-day survival kit (just in case she loses the map).

To I. M. Best, we leave the "Best" for last!

And to Camp Funny-Ha-Ha, we leave gladly!!!!